SEPTEMBER ELEGIES

BILINGUAL EDITION

ILLUSTRATIONS BY MYLES BROWN

SEPTEMBER ELEGIES

BILINGUAL EDITION

BENITO PASTORIZA IYODO
(ELEGÍAS DE SEPTIEMBRE)

TRANSLATION AND INTRODUCTION BY
BRADLEY WARREN DAVIS

Cover art: "Niña con balón" by Maité Vallejo (detail)
Collection of the translator
Cover photograph by Bradley Warren Davis

Illustrations by Myles Brown
Photographed by Joseph A. Dangler

Translation by Bradley Warren Davis
Edition prepared by Bradley Warren Davis

Elegías de septiembre, first edition, Copyright © 2003 by Benito Pastoriza Iyodo

September Elegies, bilingual edition, Copyright © 2010
by Benito Pastoriza Iyodo and Bradley Warren Davis

ISBN: Softcover   978-1-4500-3947-5

This book was printed in the United States of America.

To order additional copies of this book, contact:
Xlibris Corporation
1-888-795-4274
www.Xlibris.com
Orders@Xlibris.com
73256

September Elegies: Verses of the Unperplexed

> O trees of life, when will your winter come?
> We're never single-minded, unperplexed,
> like migratory birds. Outstript and late,
> we suddenly thrust into the wind, and fall
> into unfeeling ponds. We comprehend
> flowering and fading simultaneously.
> And somewhere lions still roam, all unaware,
> in being magnificent, of any weakness.
>
> Rainer Maria Rilke—Fourth Elegy
> *Duino Elegies*

Raison d'être

For readers who prefer exploring the breadth of poetic creation for themselves, it may be advisable to forego this introduction and begin the sojourn through *September Elegies* before the observations of others color the interpretation of this collection. One may wish to read the work, let it stand on its own and perhaps return to this prologue to compare points of departure. Upon discovering some new revelation or hidden nuance in this introductory study, the author's work can always be revisited, as poetry lends itself to bifurcated re-explorations according to the reader's precepts.

An overview

September Elegies sheds light on three components of modern life: nature, humanity and global interaction. Despite the unperplexed messages of this collection of poetry, certain of its elements present the reader with a series of intriguing conundrums, beginning with its title and continuing with the thematic variations upon which its three sections are constructed. These themes are presented in the same manner in which the author describes the morning sun: translucent, transparent and troubled.[1] The translucent light provides a hazy view of the past, transparency clearly illuminates the present and the troubled light shows a shadowy and foreboding prognosis for the future based on the inertia of the direction of contemporary society. As with most mysteries, the truths—the motives—the consequences—and the possibilities may be glimpsed, in part, by visualizing and participating in the descriptions, experiences and events presented.

Benito Pastoriza Iyodo is a poet who has also made numerous incursions into the literary genres of fiction, without losing the fundamentally poetic essence that permeates all of his works. The focus and audiences of his books have varied widely, but they all embrace an intense devotion to portraying the nuances and interrelationships of nature and man. These two themes are evident from his earliest works, including two award-winning manuscripts from his days at the University of Puerto Rico: *Gotas verdes para la ciudad (Green drops for the city)* (1975) and *El constante decir (The constant sayings)* (1976) as well as in his

---

1   From September *Elegies*, "I have touched the moon with my left eye"

first published book of poetry, *Lo coloro de lo incoloro (The color of the colorless)* which won him a Chicano-Latino Literary Prize in 1981.

Pastoriza Iyodo's first book of short stories *Cuestión de hombres (A Matter of Men)* was published in 1996. It created nine narratives, which on the surface explore the definition and role of man in society. By extension, this collection reflects an examination of the role of all "mankind" in facing the challenges of urban existence.[2] Aaron Michael Morales from Indiana State University, in his review of the bilingual edition of this book (2008), saw it as steeped in the discussion of poverty: "Indeed, while men seek identity in these stories, the issue of masculinity regularly gets trumped by the misery and cruelty of poverty—the children living in a housing project literally overflowing with refuse (one of the collection's most powerful images) or the homeless underage tunnel dwellers surviving on leftovers looted from those better off."[3] Thus, the theme of poverty proves to be one of the characteristics of man portrayed in the author's work.

Since 1996, four new works by Pastoriza Iyodo have been published: two books of poetry, a second collection of short stories and a novel, each with a different set of protagonists and subjects, but all inextricably tying nature to man and man to nature. The current book, the second of the author's works to be published in bilingual format, was originally published in

---

[2]   García, Heidi Ann. Reviews. "Pastoriza Iyodo, Benito. *Cuestión de hombres.* Bronx: Latino Press, 1996. 79 pp. ISBN 1-884-91208-7." *Chasqui: revista de literatura latinoamericana.* 35.2 (2006)

[3]   Morales, Aaron Michael. "*A Matter of Men—a review.*" *Multicultural Review* 18.2 (Summer 2009) p 55.

2003. It marks a new direction for the author by the addition of a third theme: war (and other challenges of geopolitics). The book's third section, *Bellum Venit Bellum Manet*, is appropriate for the post-9/11 era. It expands the reach of the book beyond the study of man and nature, where mankind has intervened, sometimes unwittingly, to affect the fate of the environment as well as the personal, financial or spiritual wellbeing of his fellow homo sapiens. This third component paints a broad social, economic and political backdrop upon which the microcosms of power exert their influence on both man and nature.

The Framework

The seemingly straight-forward approach of this collection of poetry contains hidden meaning, which this introduction will explore by looking at the implications of the title and the themes presented. *September Elegies* is like a vitreous mosaic with intricate details, both colored and colorless, which can be more fully experienced with the appropriate amount and angle of illumination. As the light changes in direction or intensity, so do the hues and form of the scenes portrayed. Political events, culture, human nature and social evolution provide the spectrum that irradiates this work. The first edition of the collection was published in Spanish in 2003. This bilingual edition is being published some seven years later and is the result of multiple refinements in the English version of the text. The vantage point for the translation may have shifted slightly during its development, but an essential element to unlocking the underpinnings of the work begins with a good understanding of the book's title. In order to acquire more insight into the focus of the work, it is important to understand the significance of the elegy, as that poetic form has evolved, and the inner meaning of the reference to the month of September.

September Elegies: as elegy

By its very title, *September Elegies* is a collection of elegies—a poetic form traced back to ancient Greek civilization. While the genre is often associated with praise or reminiscences relating to someone who has died, its literary definition has never been restricted to that meaning. The Greeks used the term "elegy" to refer to any poetic endeavor that was not an epic poem. Thus, its use was originally extremely broad compared to today's assumptions regarding the term.

Through the years the elegy developed a specific meter known as the elegiac couplet: in alternate lines of hexameter and pentameter. Despite this formulaic definition, even in antiquity, famous poets wrote elegies that did not conform to this metric definition.[4] Some of the greatest poets of the last several centuries utilized a much freer metric form in the delivery of their elegies. Several noted examples include: the ten elegies in Rainer Maria Rilke's *Duino Elegies,* Thomas Gray's "Elegy Written in a Country Church-Yard," "Adonais: An Elegy on the Death of John Keats" by Percy Bysshe Shelley and Walt Whitman's "When Lilacs Last in the Dooryard Bloom'd." None of these poets adhered to the

---

[4]   "Propertius is generally regarded as the unpredictable genious of elegy, flouting every tradition and convention of elegiac poetry. Ovid has always been the most popular of the elegists, exhibiting great vivacity and wit, and is unparalleled in technique." *Selected Elegies of Tibullus,* edited by W. Michael Wilson. [New York]: St. Martin's Press. 1967. p. xi.

metric scheme supposedly required of an elegy. While Gray, Shelley and Whitman all wrote elegies of lament and praise for the dead, Rilke's elegies are more philosophical and cover a wide range of themes.

According to The Concise Oxford Companion to Classical Literature: "In antiquity the elegiac metre was considered to be primarily the metre of lament, but it was used for a variety of poems, and the earliest lines we possess, written in Greece at the end of the eighth century BC, bear no resemblance to lament. Elegiac poetry was the medium for expressing personal sentiments (as distinct from narrative): for description, for exhortation to war or to virtue, for reflection on a variety of subjects, serious and frivolous, for epitaphs and laments, and for love-poems. The use of elegiacs for inscriptions to commemorate the dead seems to have become popular in the middle of the sixth century BC and persisted throughout antiquity . . . Only since the sixteenth century, has the term elegy come to denote specifically a poem of lament for an individual or a poem of serious, meditative tone."[5]

The Spanish Royal Academy's Dictionary of the Spanish Language defines the elegy as a lamentation of a deceased person or any other event worthy of tears, which can be written in tercets or in free verse.[6] Upon examining September Elegies, interconnections with the masters of the Spanish elegy are

---

[5] "elegy" The Concise Oxford Companion to Classical Literature. Ed. M.C. Howatson and Ian Chilvers. Oxford University Press, 1996. Oxford Reference Online. Oxford University Press. Eckerd College Library. 8 November 2009 <http://www.oxfordreference.com/views/ENTRY.html?subview=Main&entry=t9.e1043>

[6] "elegy" Diccionario de la Lengua Española, Edición XXI, Real Academia Española, Editorial Espasa Calpe, S.A., Madrid, 1992, p.798.

evident. To further understand the deep roots of this genre in Spanish literature and its intertextuality with the current work, the following readings are recommended: "Coplas a la muerte de su padre" by Jorge Manrique (1440-1479); "Égloga Primera" by Garcilaso de la Vega (1501-1536); "Elegía a Marta de Nevares y Carlos Félix" by Lope de Vega (1562-1635); the sonnet "Miré los muros de la patria mía" by Francisco de Quevedo (1580-1645); "En un cementario de un lugar castellano" by Miguel de Unamuno (1864-1936); "A don Francisco Giner de los Ríos" in *Elogios* (1915) by Antonio Machado (1875-1935); "Llanto por Ignacio Sánchez Mejía" by Federico García Lorca (1898-1936); and "Elegía a Ramón Sijé" by Miguel Hernández (1910-1942).

In *September Elegies*, Benito Pastoriza Iyodo follows the "free verse" Spanish tradition in the development of his elegies; however, he does not restrict them to always being laments or serious and meditative in tone. His work is more in the realm of Rilke's "Eighth Elegy," which laments the human tragedy that mankind forces upon the innocence of youth or his "Fourth Elegy," which ponders the future of nature. While many of the poems in *September Elegies* are truly laments, serious or meditative; Pastoriza Iyodo also revives the tradition of the elegy as expressing personal sentiments and commenting on the nature of mankind, whether frivolous, serious or tragic.

As Estela Porter Seale stated in the prologue of the Spanish edition of *September Elegies*, published in 2003: ". . . in light of recent world events, this work seems to be prophetic with formal Greco-Latin hues . . . . The poet is like a mirror traveling down the road reflecting the majesty and beauty of the firmaments, but also the puddles and swamps."[7]

The elegy, in its broadest sense, is an appropriate characterization of the poems in *September Elegies*. They exalt, they lament and they create implications: that if man can negatively impact nature, individuals and peoples, that mankind might also intervene to prevent further deterioration, demise, extinction, war and continued misery.

September Elegies: an autumnal journey

Months of the year have long been used as metaphors related to the cycle of life. Unlike references to December—referring to the end of life—September is more akin to a mature, yet vital, stage in life—a time of choices and change. Of course, it all depends upon whether you are looking at metaphor and philosophy from the northern hemisphere or the southern hemisphere. But for those of us in the northern portion of the globe, September signals the end of summer and the final productive yields before the onset of fall and the approaching barrenness of winter.

Summer conjures thoughts of long, lazy days of youth and abandon, often bordering on the hedonistic. Man feels invincible—immortal—with an eternity to deal with more serious matters. It is a time when many fill their lives with narcissistic pursuits, without much thought about the consequences of present actions.

7   Pastoriza Iyodo, B. *Elegías de septiembre*. [México, DF, México]: Editorial Tierra Firme. 2003. Prólogo por Estela Porter Seale. pp. 5-6.

September brings the transition from summer into fall: the time for choices that will chart individual and collective courses for the future. If the soil is tilled and seeds are planted, the next year may bring a fruitful harvest. If crops are not rotated, the soil may become unfertile, resulting in a disastrous year. Despite the frivolity of summer, September brings the opportunity for improving the chances for surviving the winter and prospering in the future. Thus *September Elegies* encompasses celebrations, laments and warnings as they deal with nature, poverty and war.

Transference of inner meaning, flow and rhythm

Poetry is perhaps the most difficult genre to translate because it hinges on the flow of images, faithful to the message of the original poem, while maintaining a literary quality in the second language. Images can be both linguistically and culturally bound, thus requiring an incursion into the psyche of the poem, exploring multiple meanings and intentions of its creator. Establishing the proper preciseness or ambiguity involves a depth of research into the anatomy of each poem and its intertextual relationship to poems within a particular section and within the entire work. This process opens the possibilities to new interpretations of the work.

Another challenge in the translation of poetry deals with the inherent nature of the two languages: Spanish and English. Spanish has a sonorous lexicon, with many words ending in vowel sounds, while the great majority of words in English end with consonants, many unvoiced and much harsher than their Spanish counterparts. This challenges the translator to create a harmonious flow to match that of the original text—no small feat. Spanish grammar also leads to an economy of words, as personal pronouns and even direct and indirect object pronouns can be incorporated into the verb form. Thus, a single verb of four or five syllables may produce a string of four or five words in English, including pronouns, articles and prepositions required for a literal translation. To address these challenges, the translation has incorporated syntactical and grammatical devices to help create a similar metric flow and rhythm to the original Spanish manuscript.

An elegiac trilogy

In *September Elegies*, Benito Pastoriza Iyodo has set into motion a trilogy based on man's impact on his world as it relates to nature, to people at the individual level and mankind at the geopolitical level. As in antiquity, the author has used Latin to create titles for each of the three sections. To preserve the mysterious and, at times, ambiguous meaning of the titles, the translation preserves them in their Latin form. Each title page also contains a quote from a different philosopher/writer, which is translated from Spanish into English. While each quote establishes a more focused view on the section's topic, it does not presage the twists and turns contained therein.

Natura Viva Natura Mortua
Nature: in the parlor of extinction

The title of the first section could, at first glance, be taken to mean "live nature—dead nature," but it can also be interpreted as "live nature—still life." The ambiguity of *natura mortua* does not mean that nature is dead, but it could imply that it is in the process of decline, as many still life paintings include the bounty of the hunt, cut flowers and fruit, all of which are dead or in some state of eventual decay.

The quote from Descartes, the 17th Century French philosopher, is particularly telling: "Nature is terrified of emptiness." These words hint at the void which may lie beyond the current precarious instability of nature as a whole. Man is a part of nature and, by extension, is also terrified of the vacuum of nothingness. Our interdependence with all aspects of our environment requires a reminder of the wonder of nature, its current plight and the vacuousness that waits if mankind does not change his current course.

Pastoriza Iyodo begins this section with a mystic, almost romantic view of nature:

> to discover nights painted by poets
> aged bards from ancient history
> is to see oneself in euphoric dawns

In the first several poems nature takes on various hues, seasons and aspects: the whites and grays of winter, the receding colors of the stars obscured by the rising sun and the multidimensional brilliance of summer. Here again, in "Kelp," Latin returns as the nomenclature for family and species of sea plants which are converted by Pastoriza Iyodo into the creatures and objects they resemble.

saccorrhiza bulbosa tentacles of an ancient sorceress
glassopteris lyallii terrified medusa
rhodymenia palmeta broccoli in flower
fucus vesiculosus petrified reef

Blue Jay Passion of Flight is the first of the poems in this section where man appears. The passion appears to go beyond the flight of the bird, focusing on the man who toils feverishly to complete his task. This poem explores the relationship of man with nature, as well as his neighbors.

of the carpenter who constructs
the fence that divides the yards
the properties the divisions
and there the blue bird jay of the night
establishes itself in its flight of passion
observing your manly labor
of a human who knows himself well
the lines the separations
the borders of Robert Frost
good fences good neighbors

And as the poem comes to a close, there is communication between man and bird that ties them inextricably together. The blue jay approaches . . .

and looks you in the face
directly in the face
spreading wings
blue and black

and you smile like an accomplice
of a single word
of a single phrase
that you know well

Man having entered the picture, the very next poem ("the earth possesses its stars") offers a transitional warning to the seas:

but caution extreme caution
with the wake of death
of petroleum that slithers in
like a snake
like a serpent
through the continental shelf
through the waves through the swells
to strangle every atom of water[8]

The result of this impending doom and man's careless contamination of the oceans is announced in "Marine Aesthetic."

so much plastic entangled with the slenderest of necks
blackened in the depth of their maritime existence
the aesthetic of the bay cloaks itself in a new color
the sullen colorless sea is reflected in one's gaze

---

[8]   The Spanish version of this poem was used as an epigraph by Rose Mary Salum in her book *Entre los espacios*. [México, D.F., México]: Editorial Tierra Firme. 2002.

Even in today's era of green consciousness, society remains oblivious to the consequences of its actions and the toll it takes on our environment.

> bitter inflamed skin of the universe
> lamenting daily for long hours
> its wounded epidermis in scabs
> as if symptoms had not erupted
> as if we were all blind
> only discerning thousands of black moons[9]

Thus, the first cycle brings the reader from the idyllic to contemporary reality, creating an awareness of the original state of nature, its fragility and mankind's irresponsibility toward its wellbeing. These elegies praise nature and, in warning, lament its not-so-gradual loss.

Paupertas Venit Paupertas Manet
Poverty: on the precipice

Literally this section could be titled *Poverty Comes Poverty Remains*, implying the intergenerational nature and hopelessness of poverty. However, it does much more than decry poverty and lament its existence and persistence. In this cycle, Pastoriza Iyodo examines what mankind denominates as good and worthwhile, and then explores the poverty of the soul as well as the poverty of the wallet. His elegies search for a reason, a cause or a responsibility for poverty. Ovid's quote—wealth has

---

[9]   From *September Elegies,* "In Red"

made me poor—seems an oxymoron until one considers that wealth is often gained through the exploitation of others or the compromise of one's own values: in either case rendering the wealthy spiritually poor.

This section opens with the theme of music: a string quartet, the blues and a bolero. The juxtaposition of the beauty of the music with the tragedy of the street creates the foundation for the lament of the loss of innocence of a little boy and a little girl, whose lives are predetermined by the destitution in which they are growing up. "A Little Girl" provides insight into such a life of poverty.

> an ancient anguish is an orphan girl
> discovering the daily deception
> linking all the perplex horizons
> colored colorless hiding from the death
> of the old rainbow the rainbow of hope
> always naked always naked

While this elegy makes reference to multiple settings throughout Latin America, the next poem, "The Boy Carries the World in His Backpack," could easily occur in any urban city. Here Pastoriza Iyodo creates the second of his more lengthy narrative poems to describe the reality of a homeless family in contrast to the other, more economically fortunate, citizens who share the space of a well-manicured park. In the following excerpt the voice changes from the third-person author to the boy's own musings.

he looks at his father with his long white beard
he looks at his mother with her discolored old dress
asking what are we in this world of nightmares
no matter what you call it the reality is the same
here alone so very alone we watch the world pass by
the high and mighty lady with her fancy Sunday bonnet
the great executive cell phone in hand solving the world's problems
the gay couple with their tiny dog like a little stuffed toy
a runner jogging on silver sidewalks to a rhythmic rap beat

And this family must endure the ultimate insult: having to feign normality to escape the long arm of the law, which might fine them or jail them for the mere status of their own economic disgrace.

no one shall be permitted to stretch out horizontally
or face a serious fine of jail time or 500 dollars
therefore one has to appear normal more than normal
one has to pass unnoticed just another family in the park
another happy family more than happy too happy in the park

Poverty is not limited to the financial, but extends itself to the sanity of the mind and spirit. In this regard, Pastoriza Iyodo examines how those who categorize themselves as intellectuals can be so very hollow in their very-well orchestrated lives. Thus is the treatise of "Good Conversation."

the close circle of idiots has gathered
to celebrate their delightful stupidities
to philosophize Plato Socrates Descartes

to discuss literature Sartre Shakespeare
to comment on art ultra postmodernism
to critique music ah Chopin how exquisite
often surrendering to the unparalleled
elegant astrological delirium of their lives

But in the poem "And What Was All That About?" Pastoriza Iyodo presents the far-reaching question: from whence cometh poverty?

because the poverty of the spirit
because the poverty of the penny
did not arrive gratuitously so easily
someone must have invented it
someone promoted it consciously
or did it simply attack us just because

This poem states what might be considered the mantra of our individualistic society: "fend for yourself as best you can / this is your problem not mine." The poem ends with the distractions designed to create some measure of escape from the unpleasant aspects of life.

I cannot avoid the terrible temptation
of sitting beside the blue-glazed river
and seeing all the royal splendor of the water
discovering its depth metrically
with eyes of a serene fish as if I had not seen
the wars the misery the hunger the death

Bellum Venit Bellum Manet
War: the power to control

The translation of the title of this section, *War Comes War Remains*, implies a constant state of war in the world, albeit an undeclared, non-military one. War is inextricably tied to power. And Espronceda's quote asking whether the world cares if there is one more cadaver, reflects the stoic indifference held by many regarding the cost of the power struggles throughout the world. In this regard, mankind finds a way to impose sadness, even in the throes of joy.

> we have heaped on every joy
> a sadness
> a region of life
> that might well
> not have been ours
> but we continue
> disuniting in every era
> casting a pall upon ourselves
> in each prism of life[10]

Another poem includes the hurling of hatred and the protection of fear as mankind pursues the disheveled urgency to simply continue living and several others prescribe the bellicose medicine that is delivered daily throughout the world: as part and parcel of a civil war, border disputes or an imperialistic attack. Pastoriza Iyodo narrates the naval attack by a mighty

---

[10]   From September Elegies, "we have maneuvered green horizons"

power upon the men, women, children and elderly citizens of another country. Its unique narrative format follows the author's penchant for a complete lack of punctuation or the use of capital letters.[11] These devices move the reader to devour the poem at a heady pace.

> ". . . throw the bait so they will come like little innocent fishes ignorant of all fault of all evilness shoot ten thousand epic missiles boom boom boom and sing profoundly alleluia alleluia I have triumphed reach for the rudder so you can sail toward the secure colorless colors of the homeland the glory of a port that has been named giant of the world and shout cheers with all the power from the depth of your lungs of how many women how many children how many old people how many men how many innocents I have thoroughly killed"[12]

This poem presents a brutal and perhaps fatalistic view of international conflict, its ramifications and consequences. However, one of the next poems, "Bravery," celebrates the many martyrs who became the catalysts for societal transformation: Martin Luther King Jr., Rosa Parks, Rigoberta Menchú and others. The poem emphasizes that one must be brave to make such fundamental changes.

> the numbed faces trapped in a thousand seas
> silence the agony of living all this filth of the sewers
> that we have created to survive the slow deterioration

---

[11]   These linguistic devices tie Benito Pastoriza Iyodo to other contemporary poets such as E. E. Cummings (e. e. cummings).

[12]   From *September Elegies*, "walk toward the boat"

because time has been measured by some few

by some few filled with coarse moral fiber

by some who have come to know the truth well

In "For a Lifetime" Pastoriza Iyodo embarks on a third narrative poem, inspired by the 9/11 attack on the World Trade Center. It reflects the despair and loss felt by so many. It is a poem that recounts a distant, intimate past and the strength of one who might be lost forever following the destruction of the twin towers. It shows the helplessness of those in the building and the vulnerability of those who watched it occur on television.

and here I am desolate

listless made an enigma of weeping

that does not comprehend life

that does not comprehend death

that does not comprehend love

that only sees through this odious luminous apparatus

people who throw themselves from the great edifice of the world

arms open legs open mouths open

floating in the air

suspended in the air

or perhaps in death

And when some escape the terror of war in their own countries and arrive in the United States, they too have memories of past strife and the knowledge that the journey is not and will never be finished, as illustrated in "Buying Dreams."

mopping floors of some omnipotent corporation or other

that invests in the death of millions

that knows of the annihilation of your friends

of the assassination of your husband your brother

. . .

in this whorehouse heaped full of stores

that shelters you forever

escaped and trapped

in the memory of your inattentive

homeland

Toward the end of this third and final cycle, Pastoriza Iyodo meditates upon mankind's desire to die simply, knowing . . . well that death / was meritorious sane well-received / that he had served some purpose.[13]

Final Observations

Benito Pastoriza Iyodo creates poetry without metric formulae, while liberating the verse through the absence of capital letters or punctuation to signal the beginning and ending of phrases. These techniques allow for varied interpretations of placing pauses when reading his work. In each of *September Elegies'* three sections, the author has included one multi-page poem that is developed in narrative form while conserving the poem-length verse as well as the poetic flow, syntax and phrasing. In *Natura Viva Natura Mortua*, "Blue Jay Passion of Flight" presents the interaction of a blue jay with a man carrying

---

[13]   From *September Elegies*, "we simply do not desire to die"

out the task of building a fence. In the original poem, the author mixes English and Portuguese in the title and English with Spanish throughout the poem. The translation, by contrast, presents both the title and the poem exclusively in English, but the contrasting languages may be observed in the original text. In *Paupertus Venit Paupertus Manet*, the narrative poem is titled "The Boy Carries the World in His Backpack," narrating the challenges of a homeless family sharing a well-groomed park with the more prosperous elements of society. In *Bellum Venit Bellum Manet*, the narrative poem chronicles the disaster of the 9/11 attack upon the World Trade Center and the tragedy of loss, fear, destruction, death and vulnerability. It reflects a simultaneous awareness of the flowering and fading of life, even as the author is unaware of the safety or peril of the poem's protagonist. These are the longest of the narrative-style poems. Another poem in the final cycle, distinguishes itself for its unique unstoppable, crescendo-like effect. "Walk toward the boat" begins innocently enough, but builds steam as the references to marine vessels increase to the caliber of a warship, which is used to attack civilians on a foreign shore, returning to its home port to celebrate a great victory over the defenseless population of another land. Here, the continuous flow of descriptive action is without pause, without punctuation, without any obstacle to the accelerating speed of the poem and the rapid completion of the mission, the destruction, the victory, the annihilation. The development of the author's focus on the subject of war is reminiscent of the transition made by Pablo Neruda from lyric poetry to his more militant verse represented by the book titled

Canto general (1950).[14] Through the third section of *September Elegies*, Benito Pastoriza Iyodo joins the ranks of poets such as Pablo Neruda and César Vallejo, who utilized poetry to portray their geopolitical world views.

Estela Porter Seale, who wrote the prologue to the Spanish-language edition of this collection, *Elegías de septiembre*, characterized the work as "a book of the indifference, of the betrayal that man shows to his fellow man, of the desecration of innocence and of nature; an entropic text of destruction and massive annihilation."[15] While this description successfully characterizes parts of the collection, it is only a fraction of the context for the entire work. The imagery of many of the poems celebrates the world and its inhabitants, even as man's intervention begins to take its toll. More than a death knell, the collection provides a beacon and a warning signal for those circumnavigating the dangerous waters where the consequences of man's lack of responsibility will surely lead to ruin.

This collection goes far beyond the nihilistic, predetermined pessimism hinted at in the first edition's prologue. This work might well be thought of as a post-modern version of Charles Dickens' *Great Expectations*—without the final chapter, a chapter that has been left to be written by the readers. In the first two sections of the collection Pastoriza Iyodo shows the virtues of nature and mankind. This praise is followed by the devastation of nature and the poverty of the individual and the soul. In

---

[14] Anderson Imbert, E. *Historia de la literatura hispanoamericana II. época contemporánea. sexta edición.* [México]: Fondo de Cultura Económica. 1974. pp. 205-206.

[15] Pastoriza Iyodo, B. *Elegías de septiembre.* [México, DF, México]: Editorial Tierra Firme. 2003. Prólogo por Estela Porter Seale. p. 6.

each case, the author demonstrates how man's intervention with nature and his lack of responsibility for the wellbeing of the environment and fellow human beings has destabilized the natural order, eroded the innocence of children and affected the health, lives and sanity of all living things. The third section focuses primarily on geopolitical friction and war, as well as their effects upon peoples, families and individuals. All three sections show a transition from description of the past to a freeze-frame picture of the current state of affairs: reflecting the warnings, transitions and interventions that bring us to the precipice. These views provide an optimistic and nostalgic representation of the past, the increasingly ominous, disinterested and devastating character of the present, and the much-feared destruction and annihilation of the future. Like the story of Pip and Estella in *Great Expectations*, intertwined lives are shaped by the intervention of men and women of power. As the protagonists become aware of their reality, as shaped by others and their own acquiescence, they come to the realization that they do have the option to make choices and change their futures.

September Elegies creates a picture of the social, economic and political fabric upon which our modern world and its notion of power are built. September is the month to make decisions on how to survive the winter and prepare for a new beginning. The elegies contained herein begin with a positive, mystic message for the future: "with letters sporadically illuminated / somewhat like a neo-human imitation / somewhat cognizant of the myth / of rainfalls in the spring." Likewise, the title of the final elegy asks the rhetorical question "And by Chance is this the End" and states: "remembering recuperating / that the hunger the misery / the war the poverty / were inventions of us all / planted well

cultivated / and meditating some little bit / upon these pages."
This opening and closing brings full circle the possibility for
reflection, choices and actions that can change the prognosis for
the future.

Bradley Warren Davis
State College of Florida

SEPTEMBER ELEGIES

I. NATURA VIVA
NATURA MORTUA

La naturaleza tiene horror del vacío

Descartes

Nature is terrified of emptiness

Descartes

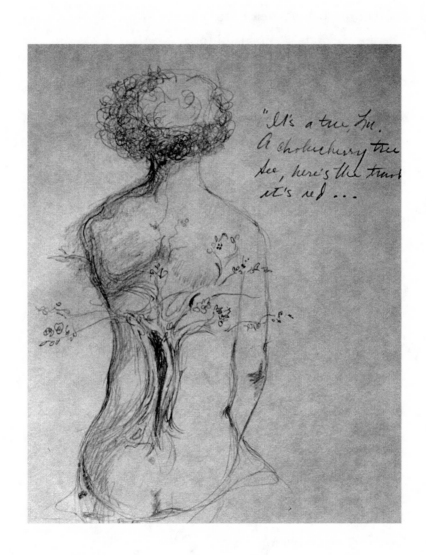

descubrir noches pintadas por poetas
bardos viejos de la antigua historia
es verse en los amaneceres de la euforia
que desconociendo van el nuevo pentagrama
de los colores matizados
por lo que santos de los santos
han denominado
lo coloro de lo incoloro
el misticismo de la transparencia
el blanco que ve su blancura
el rojo que entiende su carmesí
el verde reverdecido
en el helecho del jardín
toda la sutileza de un horizonte muerto
tragándose en la paleta del espectro
en una noche de lunas llenas
astrológicas
y perplejas
desanimadas en el sentir
con letras iluminadas esporádicamente
un tanto a la imitación neohumana
un tanto conociendo el mito
de las lluvias en primavera

to discover nights painted by poets
aged bards from ancient history
is to see oneself in euphoric dawns
that continue unaware of the novel stave
of colors tinged
by what the saints of the saints
have designated
the color of the colorless
the mysticism of transparency
the blanche that envisions its whiteness
the red that comprehends its crimson
the verdant revived
in the garden fern
all the subtleness of a dead horizon
swallowing itself in the palette of a broad spectrum
in a night of full moons
astrological
and perplex
discouraged in its emotions
with letters sporadically illuminated
somewhat like a neo-human imitation
somewhat cognizant of the myth
of rainfalls in the spring

SERAC

el barrio arrozado
se recrea en la sombra
de un horizonte profundamente
gris
más que sumido en la nieve
del espanto
espacio invertebrado de colores
donde lo inhabitado
de la esquela humana
crea susurros de profundidad
cuán de silencios ladridos
quemados por copos multiastrales
cellisca del crudo invierno
dendrita espacial del universo
circo glaciar del acantilado
de un pueblo viejo

SERAC

the snowbound region
recreates itself in the shadow
of a horizon profoundly
gray
more than submerged in the snow
out of fear
invertebrate space of colors
where the uninhabited
by human note
produces deep murmurs
as from silences howls
burned by multi-astral flakes
severe winter sleet
spatial dendrite from the universe
the cliff's glacial cirque
of an ancient people

he vivido
los colores
de lo irreal
sustancialmente
he tragado
lo incoloro
de estrellas matutinas
lanzadas
de par en par
y acá
en el poniente
quedan estáticas
desalumbradas
recogidas en el manojo
de tu calma

I have lived
the colors
of the unreal
substantially
swallowing
the colorlessness
of the morning stars
launched
two by two
and here
in the west
they remain static
blinded
gathered in a fistful
of your calm

los girasoles
giran multidimensionalizados
colores en devenir
fantasía
de lo incoloro
rojo
amarillo naranja
topacio de la mañana
plasmado en tu mano
pétalo dedo a dedo
que se han ido deshojando
sobre tu frente
encendida de verano

the sunflowers
rotate multidimensionalized
colors in formation
fantasy
of the colorless
red
yellow orange
topaz of the morning
molded in your hand
petals between fingers
which they have plucked
above your flaming
brow of summer

he sentido el cielo

a los pies

casi descendiendo

vaporoso

cada partícula

hecha agua

de una tormenta de lluvias nuevas

copiosas llenas de rabia

para saciar la sed

infinita de la tierra

que en un verde de esmeralda tranquilo

va transformándose en sauces llorosos

para pintar el ala azul

de los pitirres que se ahogan en el lago

I have felt the sky
at my feet
descending almost
vaporously
each particle
made water
from a storm of new rains
copious full of rage
to satisfy the infinite
thirst of the earth
that in a tranquil emerald green
transforms itself into weeping willows
to paint the blue wing
of the pitirres that drown in the lake

VARECH

claudea elgans elevada pluma de luz
ulva lattissima sauce de cedro
saccorrhiza bulbosa tentáculos de hechicera vieja
glassopteris lyallii medusa aterrada
rhodymenia palmeta brécol en flor
fucus vesiculosus arrecife petrificado
nitophyllum crozieri claudea elgans en solo
padinio pavonial precisamente pavo macho sin color
macrocystis pirifera alfileres de la corona etrusca

KELP

claudea elgans elevated feather of light
ulva lattissima willow of cedar
saccorrhiza bulbosa tentacles of an ancient sorceress
glassopteris lyallii terrified medusa
rhodymenia palmeta broccoli in flower
fucus vesiculosus petrified reef
nitophyllum crozieri claudia elgans in solo
padinio pavonial precisely a male peacock without color
macrocystis pirifora spires of an Etruscan crown

RELATIVO GONGORIANO

esporádicamente crear hojas amarillas
de la trasluz homosapiens invertida
es cosa relativa al tiempo de los muertos
cosa relativa al destino del caos planeado
pero
detenerse mermelado en tonalidades
crescendo de la majestuosidad natural
es descubrir una mentira descabellada
más que nada mentira paralela a sí misma
un helecho colmado en su asedio de abril
la rosa perpetua de sombra anacarada
el canto del pájaro repetido al unísono
la espina del reptil bañada en sangre
un concierto gongoriano de sentidos
un acierto de la rabia tan bien conocida

REGARDING GONGORA

sporadically creating yellow leaves
from an inverted human translucence
is somewhat akin to the hour of death
something akin to the destiny of planned chaos
but
to delay oneself suspended in tonalities
crescendo of natural majesty
is to discover a maddening deception
more a deception parallel to itself
a fern replete with April's siege
the eternal rose of lustrous hue
the bird's song repeated in unison
the reptile's spine bathed in blood
Góngora in a concert of senses
a wisdom from the rage so well known

la fiebre sabatina de los pájaros
lanzándose de punta
en la bahía hueca
del reino de los peces
donde se enerva
el sentimiento traumatizado
de tanta vida marina
tragada por la inconsistencia
del aire hecho agua
de agua convertida en muerte
en un inmenso charco gris
cementerio cotidiano
de la fauna
que baila en la paranoia
de su fiebre sabatina

the Sabbath fever of the birds
hurling themselves downward
into the empty bay
reign of the fishes
where traumatized sentiments
of prodigious marine life
become weak
swallowed by the inconsistency
of air made water
of water turned to death
in an immense gray pool
the habitual cemetery
of fauna
that dance in the paranoia
of their Sabbath fever

BLUE JAY PAIXAO DE VÔO

para Estela Porter Seale

the drop falls immaculate
into the perennials of red
pájaro azul jay of the night
sí más bien diré que sí
la gota cae inmaculada
por el desliz de tu cintura
apasionada transparentada de luz
y allí se deposita
desprovista de sueños
que le recuerden
que es mero sudor
mero trabajo de amor
una epidermis que en ti se enciende
como canto de las llamas florecidas
para recordar la fuerza la fuerza
de tus manos
de tus músculos
la pureza de tus dedos
que martillan con la furia
de un carpintero joven
del carpintero que construye
la cerca que divide los patios
las propiedades las divisiones
y allí pájaro azul jay of the night

BLUE JAY PASSION OF FLIGHT

for Estela Porter Seale

the drop falls immaculate
into the perennials of red
blue bird jay of the night
yes at least I shall say yes
the drop falls immaculate
at the curve of your waist
passionate revealed by the light
and there it deposits itself
devoid of dreams
that remind it
that it is pure sweat
a pure labor of love
an epidermis that in you burns
like a chant of flowering flames
to remember the force the strength
of your hands
of your muscles
the purity of your fingers
that hammer with the fury
of a young carpenter
of the carpenter who constructs
the fence that divides the yards
the properties the divisions
and there the blue bird jay of the night

se establece en su vuelo de pasión
observando tu labor de hombre
de humano que bien se conoce
las líneas las separaciones
las fronteras de Robert Frost
good fences buenos vecinos
y el pájaro anonadado en su vuelo
salta de cerca en cerca
hasta llegar a ti
hombre que construyes
cercas propiedades
y te mira de frente
bien de frente
esparciendo alas
azules y negras
y le sonríes como cómplice
de una sola palabra
de una sola frase
que tu bien conoces
hombre que construyes
cercas y propiedades

establishes itself in its flight of passion
observing your manly labor
of a human who knows himself well
the lines the separations
the borders of Robert Frost
good fences good neighbors
and the bird overwhelmed in its flight
hops from fence to fence
until arriving at your side
man who constructs
fences properties
and looks you in the face
directly in the face
spreading wings
blue and black
and you smile like an accomplice
of a single word
of a single phrase
that you know well
man who constructs
fences and properties

la tierra posee sus estrellas
atadas y bien contadas
en un cielo purísimo raso
de azul reluciente nacarado
ante un subsuelo marino
mítico de leyendas nuevas
y allí en espera del canto
amado milenario de sirenas
la luz logra fundirse de ébano
fundirse de coruscante asecho
pero cuidado harto cuidado
con la estela de la muerte
de un petróleo que se cuela
como una culebra
como una serpiente
por el talud continental
por las olas por las ondas
para ahorcar el átomo del agua

the earth possesses its stars
moored and well counted
in the purest cloudless sky
of a nacred iridescent blue
before a marine subsoil
mythical from new legends
and there awaiting the millinery
beloved song of the sirens
the light manages to fuse itself in ebony
to unite in a brilliant ambush
but caution extreme caution
with the wake of death
of petroleum that slithers in
like a snake
like a serpent
through the continental shelf
through the waves through the swells
to strangle every atom of water

ESTETICA MARINA

los pelícanos nadan en la doctrina estética milenaria
buscando la clara transparencia de la bahía en luces
para encontrarse con un mar de turistas engomados
mar de Copper Tone Banana Boat Clinique SPF 30+
este mar de aguas negras que se presume de todos
solo triste poseído por vergüenza mayor a la suya
por una inmensa estela de petróleo rojo azabache
flotando tranquilamente como espada luminaria
cuánta alegría de aceite peces muertos a la orilla
gaviota alcatraz espátula ibis cuervo marino garza
de todos como en botica alguno más que muerto
acompañados por latas de cerveza botellas de ron
mucho plástico enredado en lo finísimo del cuello
ennegrecido en lo profundo de su existencia marina
la estética de la bahía se viste de un nuevo color
lo incoloro tétrico del mar se refleja en la mirada

MARINE AESTHETIC

the pelicans swim in the millenary aesthetic doctrine
seeking the clear transparency of the illuminated bay
only to encounter a sea of viscid tourists
sea of Copper Tone Banana Boat Clinique SPF 30+
this sea of black waters presumably belonging to us all
alone sorrowful possessed by a shame larger than its own
by an immense wake of petroleum of red tinged obsidian
floating tranquilly like a luminary sword
such joy of oil at fish dead upon the shore
seagull the albatross duckbill ibis royal tern heron
a sample of every class some more than dead
accompanied by beer cans bottles of rum
so much plastic entangled with the slenderest of necks
blackened in the depth of their maritime existence
the aesthetic of the bay cloaks itself in a new color
the sullen colorless sea is reflected in one's gaze

los faroles marinos de la mañana
juegan horizontalmente
en el vértigo oceánico
de una transparencia verde
estimulando el danzón
de los días contados
engaño de luz y piedra
donde las algas se arrastran
en el meridional de la muerte
trueque de plata dorada
embebida en el sótano
de la noche

maritime beacons of the morning
play horizontally
in the oceanic vertigo
of a green transparency
stimulating the dance
of counted days
deception of light and rocks
where algae drag themselves along
through the zenith of death
a barter of gilded silver
absorbed in the crypt
of the night

la mermelada de nubes explotadas
baña la metrópolis en un infierno
de fuegos agomados
en un lento derretirse
de aceites caldosos
como un Dalí derramado
en la espesura de la noche
queriéndose abrigar
en las entrañas de la tierra
el cielo
acapárase a sí mismo
ya hecho volcán de Vesubio
ya hecho huracán
en el golfo de
Batabanó

the marmalade of exploded clouds
bathes the metropolis in an inferno
of viscous fires
in a slow melting
of ebullient oils
like a Dalí overflowing
in the thickness of the night
wanting to shelter itself
in the entrails of the earth
the sky
hoarding for itself
a powerful Vesuvian volcano
a mature hurricane
in the Gulf of
Batabanó

Y COMO FUE QUE DIJO

se desprende el lirismo
de su cadencia matutina
atándose al último rayo
orféico solar de estrellas
sin promesas de mañana
ni cantos hoy en zumbidos
hay que amarrarse bien
los dedos sucios las manos
para contar los astros y
cómo fue que dijo los
astros a lo lejos los astros
en el infinito para quitarse
la máscara y ver la larga
larga línea roja derretirse
por la nieve gris del crimen

AND WHAT DID HE SAY?

lyricism detaches itself
from its matutinal cadence
binding itself to the last
solar Orphic ray of stars
without promises of the morning
nor present muted chants
one must well cinch
the dirty fingers the hands
to enumerate the heavenly bodies and
what did he say the
heavenly bodies at a distance the
heavenly bodies in infinity
removing the mask to witness the long
long crimson line melted
by the gray snow of the crime

EN ROJO

amarga piel enrojecida del universo
quejándose a diario en horas largas
de su epidermis llagada en costras
como si no estallasen los síntomas
como si todos estuviésemos ciegos
sólo viendo miles de lunas negras
antes de la despiel la inocencia
la caída de la bondad severa
nadando en una luz perpetua
donde no creía verse la pena
pero aquí ahora bien entonces
la verdad la nueva verdad
la vieja verdad del hombre
la enfermedad del hombre
amarga piel del universo
a ti misma véncete rendida

IN RED

bitter inflamed skin of the universe
lamenting daily for long hours
its wounded epidermis in scabs
as if symptoms had not erupted
as if we were all blind
only discerning thousands of black moons
before the skinning the innocence
the fall of severe benevolence
swimming in a perpetual light
where one would not expect to glimpse sorrow
but here now well then
the truth the new truth
the ancient truth of man
the infirmity of mankind
bitter skin of the universe
defeat yourself exhausted

II. PAUPERTAS VENIT
PAUPERTAS MANET

La riqueza me hizo pobre

Ovidio

Wealth made me poor

Ovid

los músicos callejeros nadando en la oquedad
de una juventud minimizada en acordes de centavos
evocan un Strauss metamórfico atrapando lunas marinas
océanos perdidos con lagos claros de cisnes muertos

en un violonchelo viola violín contrabajo cuarteto
que le canta aúlla a la miseria diaria que trafica
cuarteto puramente ignorado por las hormigas humanas
permite que el son de tu fe continúe en sí mismo

permite que las lluvias en torrentes de maldad
no ahoguen los argonautas que tanto hieren las cuerdas
el toque sutil de Chopin Brahms Strauss Debussy

arrastrándose en polvo dorado por las sucias aceras
qué de las penas sentidas ignoradas por los bardos
qué de la muerte martillada en las tablas de la nota urbana

the street musicians swimming in the hollowness
of a youth minimized in chords of little value
evoke a metamorphic Strauss seizing aquatic moons
lost oceans with clear lakes of dead swans

in a double bass violoncello viola violin quartet
that sings howls to the daily misery that it traffics
a quartet altogether ignored by the human ants
allows the sound of your faith to continue within itself

allows the torrential rains of wickedness
not to drown the Argonauts who so harm the strings
the subtle touch of Chopin Brahms Strauss Debussy

dragging themselves thru golden dust on dirty sidewalks
what of the heartfelt sorrows ignored by the bards
what of death hammered on the stage of urban notes

BLUES

se cuelga la nota azul en el silencio
exigiendo mañanas de rendición total
mañanas de asunción con un WC Hardy
en espera lenta del encuentro matutino
de cadencias con Leadbelly Ma Rainey
John Hooker Billie Holiday Ella Fitzgerald
cantando a la muchachada al público exigente
del intenso azul de un ritmo ciertamente
agarrado por la tragedia sin par de la calle

BLUES

the blue note suspended itself in silence
demanding mornings of total surrender
mornings of ascension with W C Hardy
a lengthy wait for the encounter at dawn
with cadences of Leadbelly Ma Rainey
John Hooker Billie Holiday Ella Fitzgerald
singing to their groupies to the demanding audience
of the intense blue of a rhythm most certainly
embraced by the unparalleled street tragedy

place tener que sentir
la música apagada
el blues muy lejano
la danza tan de cerca
el bolero suavecito
el violonchelo en el fondo
mirarse en el riachuelo
y reconocerse de risa
en la torpe muchedumbre
que ha conocido
el desfile de los payasos
el baile de los enamorados

it pleases having to feel
the subdued music
the very distant blues
dancing ever so close
the bolero's suave sway
the cello in the background
to see yourself in the stream
and recognize your own laugh
among the awkward crowd
that has encountered
the parade of clowns
the waltz of lovers

UN NIÑO

un niño suave tejido en rizos de barro
rizos de escorpión rizos de telarañas
ha visto la visión de lo verde nacer
cerca de su leve costado en puños
anudado a cada aparente origen
torcido en geométricos ostionoides
de un supuesto relieve casto de arenas
de una pureza más que inventada
por el hombre que se televisa en corbata
en camisa blanca planchada de Gucci
niño que se va tragando la miseria
en que vive orina crece muere
un niño tejido en rizos de barro
más bien comiendo vomitando nadando
un niño de rizos escorpión
un niño de telarañas
en el fango de la desgracia inventada

A LITTLE BOY

a soft boy with braided curls of clay
curls of scorpions curls of spider webs
has seen the vision of the green being born
close to his fragile flank tied in knots
entangled in each apparent origin
twisted in geometric oyster-shapes
presumably a chaste relief of sands
of a purity more than invented
by the man on television dressed in a tie
in a white ironed Gucci shirt
a boy continues swallowing the misery
in which he lives urinates grows up dies
a boy braided in curls of clay
in reality eating vomiting swimming
a boy of scorpion curls
a boy of spider webs
in the muck of an invented disgrace

UNA NIÑA

un viejo dolor es una niña huérfana
descubriendo la cotidiana mentira
de un hambre de agua con azúcar
casi descalza por los barrios de Lima
los cerros de Caracas los ranchos del DF
los arrabales de Tegucigalpa los caseríos
de La Paz San Juan la mugre de la pobreza
en un Buenos Aires querido en un Santiago
que tanto se odia se ama por la miseria
de las miserias en Quito en Asunción en Río
con las favelas hasta las narices una Habana
en desecho un Santo Domingo muerto
una Managua arrastrándose en las ruinas
una Ciudad de Panamá ahogada en drogas
un San Salvador en pura purita desgracia
Guatemala Ciudad bomba viene bomba va
Montevideo en el panorama del infortunio
un viejo dolor es una niña huérfana
descubriendo la cotidiana mentira
atando todos los horizontes perplejos
coloros incoloros agazapados de muerte
al viejo arco iris al arco iris de la esperanza
siempre desnuda siempre desnuda

A LITTLE GIRL

an ancient anguish is an orphan girl
discovering the daily deception
of a hunger for sugared water
almost barefoot in the barrios of Lima
the hillsides of Caracas the shanties of Mexico City
the Tegucigalpa slums the squalid projects
of La Paz San Juan the filth of poverty
in a cherished Buenos Aires in a Santiago
so much loved and hated for its misery
of the miseries in Quito in Asuncion in Rio
with its unending favelas a Havana
crumbling a Santo Domingo devoid of life
a Managua shuffling through its ruins
a Panama City drowned in drugs
a San Salvador in total and utter disgrace
Guatemala City besieged by bombs
Montevideo in the panorama of misfortune
an ancient anguish is an orphan girl
discovering the daily deception
linking all the perplex horizons
colored colorless hiding from the death
of the old rainbow the rainbow of hope
always naked always naked

EL NIÑO LLEVA EL MUNDO
EN SU MOCHILA

el niño lleva el mundo en su mochila
un niño rubio de ojos sutilmente azules
lleva al mundo con una cara despintada
con una tristeza arrancada de la tristeza
lleva en su cara polvo gris de las ciudades
el niño lleva su mundo en la mochila
pasta de dientes toalla sucia pantalones zurcidos
camiseta que dice Magic Kingdom Disney World
un oso peluche negro que se encontró en la basura
calcetines de anteayer calzoncillos que no llegan a mañana
y la luna llena anaranjada está plantada en el cielo
como un gran obelisco inventado por los dioses
y a lo lejos se dibuja la fuente de hermosos colores
jardines con rosales jardines con jasmines
el parque es una preciosidad de banquetas antiguas
con su hierro fornido labrado y bien decorado
el lago la inmensidad del lago la transparencia del lago
los cisnes en el lago los patitos negros en el lago
y la noche terriblemente estrellada de azulejos
con el niño agarrado al peluche negro
que mira a su padre de una barba larguísima y blanca
que mira a su madre de un vestido descolorado y viejo
preguntando qué somos en este mundo de pesadillas

THE BOY CARRIES THE WORLD IN HIS BACKPACK

the boy carries the world in his backpack
a blonde boy with eyes of subtle blue
bears the world with an ashen face
with a sadness snatched from a greater sadness
his face wears the gray dust of city streets
the boy carries his world in the backpack
a tube of toothpaste dirty towel mended pants
a T shirt reading Magic Kingdom Disney World
a black stuffed bear that he found in the dumpster
two day old socks underwear that won't make it to tomorrow
and the orange full moon is planted firmly in the sky
like a gigantic obelisk invented by the gods
and at a distance a fountain with beautiful colors
gardens with roses gardens with jasmines
the park is lovely with its old-fashioned benches
of ornate wrought iron elaborately designed
the lake the immensity of the lake the transparency of the lake
the swans in the lake the little black ducks in the lake
and the terribly starry night of glistening tiles
with the little boy clinging to his stuffed black bear
he looks at his father with his long white beard
he looks at his mother with her discolored old dress
asking what are we in this world of nightmares

destechados desahuciados vagabundos homeless
que más da el término si el hecho es el mismo
aquí solitos bien solitos miramos el mundo pasar
la señora señorona con su gran sombrero de domingo
el gran ejecutivo con celular a la mano resolviendo el mundo
la pareja gay con su perro perrito de juguete
el corredor trotando las plateadas aceras a ritmo de rap
la puta fina que no debe ser descubierta por la poli
los niños hermosos vestidos en hilo blanco
las niñas lindísimas vestidas en rosado antiguo
las parejas de enamorados bien enamorados
y el niño busca en su mochila el mundo que le ha tocado
una sábana desvencijada una almohadilla que da vergüenza
para dormir dónde cuándo cómo y con qué propósito
porque la ley estipula claramente que en los parques
no se ha de recostar el cuerpo horizontalmente
que es una multa grave de cárcel o 500 dólares
por lo tanto hay que verse normal más que normal
hay que pasar por desapercibido otra familia en el parque
otra familia más que feliz demasiado feliz en el parque
le explica le aclara le recuerda su padre su madre
el niño que lleva su mundo en la mochila
no entiende de leyes ni reglas ni patrones
sólo ve el cisne deslizándose ligeramente por el agua
los sauces los pinos los ciprés los robles ensombrecidos
y él con un sueño profundísimo de lejanas estrellas
con un hambre vieja y pesada casi milenaria
y su madre y su padre pellizcándolo que no se duerma
que mire a los patitos que juegue con su oso negro

destitute displaced evicted vagabonds homeless
no matter what you call it the reality is the same
here alone so very alone we watch the world pass by
the high and mighty lady with her fancy Sunday bonnet
the great executive cell phone in hand solving the world's problems
the gay couple with their tiny dog like a little stuffed toy
a runner jogging on silver sidewalks to a rhythmic rap beat
the classy whore avoiding the vigilant eye of the cops
the handsome little boys dressed in white linen
the precious little girls dressed in soft antique pink
the pairs of lovers hand in hand so very much in love
and the boy hunts in his backpack the world that he's been dealt
a threadbare tattered sheet and a pillow he's ashamed of
to sleep where when how and for what purpose
because the law clearly stipulates that in the parks
no one shall be permitted to stretch out horizontally
or face a serious fine of jail time or 500 dollars
therefore one has to appear normal more than normal
one has to pass unnoticed just another family in the park
another happy family more than happy too happy in the park
his parents explain clarify and remind him
the boy who carries his world in his backpack
does not understand laws nor rules nor standards
he only watches the swan lightly gliding across the water
weeping willows the pines the cypress trees the shady oaks
and he with the deep sleepiness of distant stars
with a persistent weighty hunger almost millenary
and his mother and father pinching him so he won't fall asleep
look at the ducklings play with your black bear

que mire a la gran gran luna anaranjada llena
que busque su mundo en la pequeña mochila verde
pero que por favor no se duerma
por favor no se duerma
no se duerma

look at the great orange full moon
look for your world in your small green backpack
but please don't fall asleep
please don't fall asleep
don't fall asleep

un ojo ha visto la pena de la locura
tirarse por el mundo más que descalza
rogando limosnas en cada esquina sucia
prostituyendo la piel de la cintura agria
elaborando el deshacer cotidiano como si
aquello fuese humana tristeza de centavo
greñas largas de pacotilla en segunda
demencia gris extendida por las nubes
la loca del barrio el loco borracho del bar
que fácil decirlo sólo más que decirlo
cuando muy cómodo se sienta ante el sofá
la novela la telenovela para vivirla bien
balanceada cordura de la buena vida
mientras la locura se hace locura
y la muerte se nos cuela por los recovecos
de la conciencia tejiendo la trampa de la vida
de un acervo más que rendido en cuentas

an eye has seen the sorrow of madness
wandering the globe more than barefoot
begging for alms on every dirty street corner
prostituting the flesh of its bitter waist
elaborating the daily perdition as though
it were a few cents worth of human sadness
long shocks of second-rate hair
gray dementia extended to the clouds
the neighborhood madwoman the crazy drunk in the bar
how easy it is to say even more saying it
when one is sitting comfortably on a couch
the novel the soap opera to live well
the balanced sanity of the good life
while madness begets madness
and death slowly seeps into the recesses
of the conscience weaving a life of deceit
of a hoarding more than what we are due

una noche de invierno de frío invierno
desde la ventana rota de azulejos nuevos
una vela una alcoba una recámara vacía
una frazada un edredón una almohada
unas botas viejas unos calcetines negros
he visto un hombre llorar solo con su pena
bien solito que lloraba con tanta lágrima
que harto le sobraba para que la humanidad
llorase con él en aquella esquina despiadada
la esquina donde la basura del hombre moderno
le llega hasta el cuello de la desgracia humana
la nieve naranja más bien una nieve roja de sangre
bañaba su rostro bañaba el pecho bañaba la cintura
y el hombre se quedó quietecito bien quietecito
esperando que la muerte se le filtrara por los codos

a winter night a cold winter night
from a broken window of glazed tiles
a candle a chamber an empty bedroom
a blanket a down comforter a pillow
a pair of old boots some black socks
I have seen a man cry alone in sorrow
very much alone crying so many tears
that he had enough for all humanity
to cry with him on that pitiless corner
the corner where the trash of modern man
reaches up to one's neck in human disgrace
the orange snow more a snow red with blood
bathed his face bathed his chest bathed his waist
and the man stayed still he remained quite still
waiting for death to filter through his flesh

BUENA CONVERSACION

la sarta de idiotas se han reunido
para festejar sus bellas estupideces
filosofar Platón Sócrates Descartes
hablar literatura Sartre Shakespeare
comentar arte ultra postmodernismo
criticar música mira Chopin que bonito
comúnmente se entregan al fino delirio
astrológico sin par de sus existencias
eres aries cáncer yo escorpión piscis
mi luna leo sabes sagitario ascendente
mucho refinamiento nada de fealdades
cómo te llamas mira que lindo tu nombre
como mítico como mitológico como mm . . .
atándose alcohólicamente atontados
a una vodka un ron un tequila un vino
y comentan que bien la están pasando
que bueno ha sido el hermoso destino
que bien hemos planeado nuestras vidas
y que lindo la estamos pasando

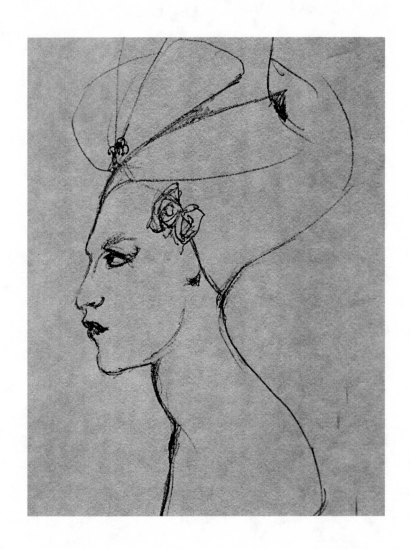

GOOD CONVERSATION

the close circle of idiots has gathered
to celebrate their delightful stupidities
to philosophize Plato Socrates Descartes
to discuss literature Sartre Shakespeare
to comment on art ultra postmodernism
to critique music ah Chopin how exquisite
often surrendering to the unparalleled
elegant astrological delirium of their lives
you are Aries Cancer I am Scorpio Pisces
my moon in Leo with Sagittarius ascending
refinement abounds nothing of ugliness
comment vous appelez-vous what a beautiful name
how mystic as if mythological like hmm . . . .
anchoring themselves stupefied in alcohol
to vodka a rum tequila a glass of wine
and they rave what a good time they are having
how wonderfully beautiful their destiny has been
how well we have planned our lives
and what a beautiful time we are having

Y ¿COMO FUE LA COSA?

será tanta miseria desgracia
una casualidad que nos cayó
de puritita casualidad del cielo
porque la pobreza del espíritu
porque la pobreza del centavo
no nos llegó gratuita tan fácil
alguien se la habrá inventado
alguien la promulgó a conciencia
o simplemente se nos dio así no más
porque así son las desgracias del hombre
las entrañas de la conciencia me dicen
que así no fue la cosa la cuestión en mano
alguien dijo aquí te parto la vida
arréglatelas como tú puedas
éste es tu problema y no el mío
más aún con tanta sobrada penuria
en el mundo de la intransigencia
no puedo evitar la terrible tentación
de sentarme frente al río de azulejos
y mirar tanta agua real esplendorosa
descubrir la profundidad métricamente
con ojos de pez sereno como quien no vio
la guerra la miseria el hambre la muerte

AND WHAT WAS ALL THAT ABOUT?

could it be that so much misery disgrace
was a mere coincidence that befell us
by pure chance from the heavens
because the poverty of the spirit
because the poverty of the penny
did not arrive gratuitously so easily
someone must have invented it
someone promoted it consciously
or did it simply attack us just because
thus is the nature of human disgraces
the entrails of my conscience tell me
that it wasn't like that the matter at hand
someone set out to make life miserable
fend for yourself as best you can
this is your problem not mine
even more with so much destitution
in this world of intransigence
I cannot avoid the terrible temptation
of sitting beside the blue-glazed river
and seeing all the royal splendor of the water
discovering its depth metrically
with eyes of a serene fish as if I had not seen
the wars the misery the hunger the death

contarme unas falacias de ayuno temprano
unas mentirillas de humano arrepentido
al punto en son y descubrir el hecho
de la desgracia un tanto borrado

telling myself some tall tales of early fasting
some little lies of a repentant human being
to the point of song and discovering the fact
of a tragedy somewhat vanquished

aúlla una pena lentamente
a torrentes de esófagos
y estómagos vacíos
porque el hambre
de los pueblos nuevos
sigue bien presente
calando en la miseria
del hombre moderno
como si pudiese morder
la tristeza la amargura
en tres cantos de dolor
despedazándose la vida
nota de cada fuego
nota de cada ser
consumiéndose en el oprobio

a sorrow howls languidly
in torrents from throats
and empty stomachs
because the hunger
of newborn nations
continues ever present
dredging in the misery
of modern man
as though it could bite
the sadness the bitterness
in three cantos of pain
splitting life asunder
a note from every fire
a note from every being
consuming itself in scorn

COLOMBIA, BRASIL, INDIA, ETC.

diría hoy se ha violado el alma
de un niño cruzando la calle
la sucia esquina de la desgracia
atado glacialmente terriblemente
a la tierra a la humanidad al suelo
que lo presenció en el espacio
en el contorno de su cuerpo
y razgó la traspiel del niño
para asegurarse que quedó
bien muertecito bien muertecito
y allí durmió violado ultrajado
desmembrado dije desmembrado
una infancia quebrada en puntos
una secuela bien tramada
un tiroteo de las cabezas
el rompecabezas de la inocencia

COLOMBIA, BRAZIL, INDIA, ETC.

one could say that today crossing the street
the soul of a young boy has been violated
the filthy corner of disgrace
bound terribly glacier-like
to the earth to humanity to the soil
that witnessed him in space
in the contour of his body
and it slashed deep within the boy's skin
to make certain that he was most assuredly
and completely dead quite dead
and there he lay violated insulted
dismembered yes dismembered
an infancy shattered into pieces
an outcome well-planned
a summary execution to the head
the challenging puzzle of innocence

III. BELLUM VENIT
BELLUM MANET

Que haya un cadáver más, ¿qué importa al mundo?

> Espronceda

That there be one cadaver more, what does it matter to the world?

> Espronceda

UN MAPA QUE DE SUR SE ME REQUIEBRA

sentándome estoy con un costado de pretéritos
bordando si acaso unos futurismos de espectros
con un pentagrama de colores en sombra
pero cómo no sentir la desgracia medida
el orbe que pierde su cause de siglos
en una pena tintada de gris naranja
cómo no entregarme a la lágrima sucia
de la esquina de la calle cualquiera
acaso cómo no hacerlo sin un espejo
bien enterrado recordando la mentira
la historia de las historias
la mentira de las historias
mirando un mapa que de sur
se me requiebra por las esquinas
un mapa suelto cortado
por el ombligo de su madre

A MAP THAT FROM THE SOUTH CRUMBLES UPON ME

here I am sitting with a core of preterits
embroidering perhaps a few spectral futurisms
with a stave of colors in the shadows
but how not to feel the measured disgrace
the sphere that loses its course of centuries
in a sorrow tinged an orange-gray
how not to surrender to the soiled tear
of the corner of any street anywhere
perchance how not to do it without a mirror
well buried remembering the lie
the history made of stories
the falsehood of the stories
looking at a map that from the south
crumbles upon me from the corners
a map loose severed
from its mother's center

hemos conducido verdes horizontes
por nuestras vidas
algunos por preferencia
han sido rojos
hemos colmado en cada alegría
una tristeza
una región de vida
que muy bien
no podría ser nuestra
pero nos seguimos
desuniendo en cada tiempo
ennegreciéndonos
en cada cristal de vida
cosa de que el tono
siga tierra
tierra quevediana
tierra de pena

we have maneuvered green horizons
throughout our lives
some by preference
have been red
we have heaped on every joy
a sadness
a region of life
that might well
not have been ours
but we continue
disuniting in every era
casting a pall upon ourselves
in each prism of life
so that the hue
remains earth
Quevedo-like earth
an earth of sorrow

LA COSA NO ES CONMIGO

presumir de viento

con raíces alocadas

con parámetros desalineados

presumir de viento

con sueños amontonados

presumir de viento

para arrojar el odio

para arropar el miedo

para no comprometernos

presumir de viento

para una vez más

recordar

la urgencia

descabellada que tenemos

de seguir

viviendo

IT'S NONE OF MY CONCERN

presuming to be wind
with demented roots
with misaligned parameters
presuming to be wind
with amassed dreams
presuming to be wind
to hurl hatred
to protect fear
to not commit ourselves
presuming to be wind
to once again
remember
the disheveled urgency
we possess
to continue
living

EL AYUNO

relativamente ayuno días de pesares
para tostar y tragarme la esperanza
con mermelada de mucha ignorancia
asesinarla de a poquito poco a poco
con dos tiros que duelan en exceso
o acaso tres para dar con el acierto
digerir la felicidad la alegría la fe
no es el lema constante del día
más bien el cúmulo de agravios
en el torax parece tomar un desvío
y recetar con gran sabiduría de siglos
tres toneladas de dolor
para el mundo
por cada día
por cada guerra
por cada ser

THE FAST

relatively I fast days of sorrows
to toast and swallow hope
with marmalade of much ignorance
murdering it little by little by little
with two gunshots that hurt to excess
or perhaps three just to make certain
to digest happiness joy faith
is not the constant motto of the day
it's more likely the host of affronts
in the thorax that seems to take a detour
and prescribes with great wisdom of the centuries
three tons of pain
for the world
for each day
for each war
for each being

caminar hacia la barca hacia el barco hacia la lancha hacia el bote hacia el velero hacia el buque de guerra tomar el pedal tomar los remos tomar las velas tomar las armas navegar con rumbo donde presientas el conflicto guiándote por las estrellas por el poniente en una circunferencia de 400 metros más bien 500 metros para estar seguro y pensar en la nube que tienes que observar en la estrella en la luna llena que te ha de orientar la brújula el sonar el radar tirar el anzuelo que vengan como pececitos inocentes ignorantes de toda culpa de toda maldad disparar diez mil misiles terriblemente épicos boom boom boom y cantar profundamente aleluya aleluya he triunfado alcanzar el timón para ponerte a bogar hacia los colores incoloros seguros de la patria la gloria de un puerto que ha nominado gigante del mundo y gritar a vivas con mucha fuerza pulmón adentro que muchas mujeres que muchos niños que muchos viejos que muchos hombres que muchos inocentes he requetematado walk toward the boat toward the ship toward the dingy toward the skiff toward the sailboat toward the warship take the pedal take the oars take the sails take the weapons navigate on the bearing where you have a presentiment of the conflict guiding yourself by the stars by the west wind in a circumference of 400 meters even better 500 meters just to be sure and think about the cloud that you must observe in the star in the full moon that will position you the compass the sonar throw the bait so they will come like little innocent fishes ignorant of all fault of all evilness shoot ten thousand terribly epic missiles boom boom boom and sing profoundly alleluia alleluia I have triumphed reach for the rudder so you can sail toward the secure colorless colors of the homeland the glory of a port that has been named giant of the world and shout cheers with all the power from the depth of your lungs of how many women how many children how many old people how many men how many innocents I have thoroughly killed

EL PLAN TORCIDO

bueno he sido con todos los males de males
que pisando siento debajo de las suelas en lodo
las calles grises sucias empobrecidas destartaladas
llenas de odio de guerra de hambre vergonzosa
devuelven el suspiro un aliento torcido de pesares
pisando voy la sangre sobre la tierra de los muertos
los cadáveres de los niños la niñas violadas porque sí
porque nos dio la real gana de hacerlo somos machos
soldados machos bien machos más que machos con
fusiles bayonetas dagas puñales granadas ametralladoras
para matar a los hombres dejarlos bien muertecitos
porque se nos torció el plan altruista de los altos montes
porque ahora somos los asesinos los violadores la escoria

THE WARPED PLAN

I have been good with all the evils of evils
that treading through muck I feel beneath my soles
the gray dirty streets impoverished dilapidated
full of hatred of war of shameful hunger
return the sigh the warped bravery of regrets
I go trudging in the blood on the earth of the dead
the cadavers of the boys the raped girls because yes
because we simply felt like doing it we are machos
macho soldiers very machos more than machos with
rifles bayonets daggers knives grenades machine guns
to kill the men to leave them very much dead
because our altruistic plan of the high mountains became warped
because now we are the assassins the rapists the scum of the earth

BRAVURA

los movimientos delfinizados de los mártires
que se abren las venas hasta sangrarse de pena
van conociendo cuanta mentira descabellada
nos hemos inventado para acallar la verdad
de las verdades que sólo ellos presentían
Martin Luther King Rosa Parks Malcolm X
César Chávez Rigoberta Menchú Lolita Lebrón
abren la puerta roja liberada del tiempo muerto
caminando liberándose en cada gesto de palabra
no sentándose en el asiento trasero de la ignominia
filosofar hasta cansarse en develar la negra trama
hambre más que hambre hasta ver el cielo desgarrarse
bala viene bala va esquivando la muerte en la esquina
prisión de hierro hasta que Dios diga basta y baje el dedo
los rostros entumecidos atrapados de mil mares
callan la agonía de vivir toda esta escoria de alcantarillado
que hemos creado para sobrevivir el deterioro lento
porque el tiempo se ha medido por unos cuantos
por unos cuantos bravos llenos de agallas toscas
por unos que muy bien han conocido la verdad

BRAVERY

the dolphinized movements of the martyrs
that open their veins until they bleed out from grief
they come to know how much of a disheveled lie
we have invented to silence the truth
of the truths that only they perceived
Martin Luther King Rosa Parks Malcolm X
César Chávez Rigoberta Menchú Lolita Lebrón
they open the red door liberated from dead time
walking liberating themselves in each expression of word
not sitting in the back seat of ignominy
philosophizing to exhaustion to reveal the black plot
hunger more than hunger until seeing the heavens shatter
bullets coming and going dodging death on the corner
a prison of iron until God says enough and his finger points down
the numbed faces trapped in a thousand seas
silence the agony of living all this filth of the sewers
that we have created to survive the slow deterioration
because time has been measured by some few
by some brave few filled with coarse moral fiber
by some few who have come to know the truth well

he tocado la luna con mi ojo izquierdo
de tres maneras he visto el sol mañanero
translúcido transparente trastocado
en una suave hora de cualquier verano
con vientos pasajeros de la noche fría
un día tan hermoso que merece poema
poesía de la más cursi imaginable posible
entonces por qué me empeño en la guerra
en el recuerdo la pesadilla el desaforo
de la bala ensangrentada metida en el pecho
en la panza en la costilla en lo más adentro
de la espina dorsal donde duele tanto tanto
por qué no salvar lo coloro de lo incoloro
convertir la sangre en flor convertir las moscas
que zumban a la mirada del muerto en mariposas
por qué no me entierro en la poesía de la conspiración

I have touched the moon with my left eye
in three ways I have seen the morning sun
translucent transparent troubled
in the sweet hour of any summer
with passing winds of a cold night
a day so beautiful that it merits a poem
the most affected poetry possibly imaginable
then why do I insist on war
on the memory of the nightmare the outrage
the bloody bullet piercing the chest
in the stomach in the rib in the deepest part
of the spinal column where it hurts so very much
so why not save the color of the colorless
convert the blood into a flower convert the flies
that buzz at the sight of the dead into butterflies
why not bury myself in the poetry of the conspiracy

lluevo lágrimas
todos los días
antes de ver la
aurora
antes de ver
la guerra
antes de ver
la muerte
pienso en la tarde
de un descontento
de un fuego
de un desastre
y
lluevo lágrimas
todos
los días

I rain tears
every day
before seeing
the dawn
before seeing
the war
before seeing
death
I think in the afternoon
of a discontent
of a fire
of a disaster
and
I rain tears
every
day

PARA TODA UNA VIDA

para Olguita

cuando pienso en su pequeño abriguito de flecos
en los rizos que le caen al hombro
y sus enormes ojos de niña bruja
que me dicen meni bye bye
que me dice que quiere paseo
que quiere conocer al mundo
recuerdo cuánto la quiero
cuánto la quiero
cuánto quiero a la niña
de los pies ligeros
que me abraza con todo su anhelo
que me dice que me quiere
más allá del cielo
más allá del cielo
que me abraza con toda su inocencia
con toda su ternura
con todo su amor de niña bruja
que me hechiza todo
de los pies al pelo
esta criatura de dos pies y medio
que es toda dulzura
un encanto del cual soy esclavo
para toda una vida
para toda una vida

FOR A LIFETIME

for Olguita

when I think of her little fringed coat
of the curls that fall upon her shoulders
and the enormous eyes of this bewitching girl
that tell me "meni bye-bye"
that tell me she wants to go for a walk
that she wants to explore the world
I remember how much I love her
how much I love her
how much I love this little girl
with two swift feet
who embraces me with all her zeal
who tells me that she loves me
far beyond the heavens
far beyond the heavens
who embraces me with all her innocence
with all her tenderness
with all the love of this beguiling girl
that enchants me completely
from head to toe
this creature two and a half feet tall
who is all sweetness
a spell to which I am slave
for a lifetime
for a lifetime

y aquí me siento

ante el aparato luminoso

que me dice me grita

me mata me remata

que el gran edificio del mundo

se ha desmoronado

se ha caído en llamas

en humo en polvo

en gases

con mi niña bruja

con mi niña de los encantos

que descubrió el bye bye de su vida

que se hizo mujer

tan bella tan fuerte tan hermosa tan valiente

en esa gran metrópoli del infiero

que tanto temí para ella

pero ella siempre tan fuerte

tan dispuesta a su bye bye

de la vida

y yo tan cobarde tan débil

queriendo que no dejara de ser

la niña de los rizos

la niña de los ojos brujos

la niña que tanto me quiere

como bien diría ella

tanto tanto tanto

y aquí estoy desolado

apagado hecho un enigma de llantos

que no comprende la vida

no comprende la muerte

and here I sit
before this luminous apparatus
that tells me yells at me
kills me kills me again
that the great edifice of the world
has crumbled
has fallen in flames
in smoke in dust
in gases
with my little enchantress
with my little girl who casts spells
that discovered the bye-bye of her life
who became a woman
so beautiful so strong so captivating so valiant
in this great metropolis of the inferno
which I so feared for her
but she was always so strong
so ready for her bye-bye
of life
and I so cowardly so weak
wanting her not to cease being
the little girl with the curly hair
the little girl with the bewitching eyes
the little girl that loves me so much
as she would say
so much so much so much
and here I am desolate
listless made an enigma of weeping
that does not comprehend life
that does not comprehend death

no comprende el amor
sólo ve por este odioso luminoso aparato
gente que se tira del gran edificio del mundo
brazos abiertos piernas abiertas bocas abiertas
flotando en el aire
suspendidos en el aire
o acaso la muerte
y yo sin mi niña
sin mi meni bye bye
sin el abriguito de flecos
sin los ojos de brujita
que me digan
te quiero
tanto tanto tanto

that does not comprehend love
that only sees through this odious luminous apparatus
people who throw themselves from the great edifice of the world
arms open legs open mouths open
floating in the air
suspended in the air
or perhaps in death
and me without my little girl
without my "meni bye-bye"
without the little fringed coat
without the bewitching eyes
that tell me
I love you
so much so much so much

COMPRANDO SUEÑOS

vives desolada como un antiguo faro oculto en la selva
donde la guerra quebradiza y ya sin canto
te ve cubierta de ojeras de una nocturna mañana
desayunando tu hamburguesa plástica que se perfora en balas
comprando en gringolandia los regalos navideños
de unos sueños que te inventas a cuesta de sangre en pesadillas
te remontas al combate las bombas el secuestro
porque te acuerdas del tío asesinado
del primo torturado en una noche temprana como ésta
de las veces mil
que corriste a refugiarte en el prostíbulo de la esquina
para no ver la muerte de cerca
para salvar las crías
esos que lloran y gritan con la madrugada
que no comprenden los presentes de un santo gringo navideño
y aquí trasvuelas las horas largas y contadas
trapeando pisos de no sé que corporación omnipotente
que invierte en la muerte de los millones
que conoce del aniquilamiento de tus amigos
del asesinato de tu marido tu hermano
de un humo bélico que se confunde
en los ojos trastocados de un pasado
y este presente que te muerde ferozmente
que no te permite olvidar aquello
resignarte a lo cotidiano de la vida

BUYING DREAMS

you live desolate like an ancient lighthouse hidden in the jungle
where the war fragile and without a canto
sees you covered with dark predawn circles under the eyes
breakfasting on plastic hamburgers perforated by bullets
buying Christmas gifts in gringoland
from self-invented dreams at the cost of bloody nightmares
you go back to the combat the bombs the kidnapping
because you remember your uncle's assassination
the tortured cousin on an early evening like this
of the thousands of times
that you ran for refuge to the brothel on the corner
to not see death so close
to save the children
that begin crying and screaming with the dawn
who don't understand the presents of the gringo Saint Nick
and here you drift back to the long endless hours
mopping floors of some omnipotent corporation or other
that invests in the death of millions
that knows of the annihilation of your friends
of the assassination of your husband your brother
of the bellicose smoke that becomes confused
in the taciturn eyes of the past
and this present that bites you ferociously
not permitting you to forget
resigning yourself to the daily routine of life

simplemente comerte este trastorno de alimento

que llaman hamburguesa con queso

pero no

se te requiebra la vida descocida

y la muerte es el comienzo

donde el sitio del dolor se incrementa

con este regalo navideño que se desconoce

en la envoltura de llamas rojas

de una sangre antigua vieja milenaria

de un fuego que te abruma profundamente

de los estallidos de la guerra que no se calla

porque no has llegado

porque sigues allí

con la muerte a tu lado

en este prostíbulo de tiendas de montones

que te refugia para siempre

escapada y atrapada

en la memoria de tu suelo

desmemoriado

simply eating this meaningless nourishment
called a hamburger with cheese
but no
your unsown life collapses upon you
and death is the beginning
where the place of pain increases
with this Christmas gift unrecognizable
in its wrapping paper of red flames
of blood ancient aged millenary
of fire that overwhelms you profoundly
of the explosions of war that will not be silent
because you have not arrived
because you are still there
with death by your side
in this whorehouse heaped full of stores
that shelters you forever
escaped and trapped
in the memory of your inattentive
homeland

ATREVIMIENTO

por qué se ha de repetir el mismo poema
acaso en una simple lectura de vocablos
hojeada de palabras hartas masticadas
en el tórax de una conciencia revestida
el tiempo se futuriza en el sustantivo
como quien va midiendo la vida
relatando necedades del universo
ufanándose en desperdiciar el teclado
prácticamente perder práctico provecho
en escribir líneas didácticas en su punto
y coma interrogación la exclamación
que algo digan que algo expliquen
que en algo se vea la gris verdad
la verdad que ya todos nos conocemos

DARING

why should we repeat the same poem
by chance in a simple reading of vowels
a skimming of words well masticated
in the thorax of a cloaked conscience
time becomes futuristic in the noun
like one who continually measures life
relating the foolishness of the universe
boasting of wasting the keyboard
practically losing the practical benefit
of writing lines didactic in their point
and comma question exclamation
that they say something explain something
that in something the gray truth is seen
the truth that we already know

simplemente no deseamos morir
con poco aire en la garganta
como quien recibe una flor
imprevista de un amante fugaz
cazar cada estrella magnetizarla
en aromas y sentirla muy de cerca
morir deseamos simplemente
humedeciendo los dedos al aire
del que bien dejó algo otorgado
del que bien supo que la muerte
fue meritoria sana bien recibida
de que para algo sirvió

we simply do not desire to die
with little air in our throats
like one who receives a flower
unexpected from a fleeting lover
hunting each star magnetizing it
in aromas and feeling it so very close
we desire to die simply
dampening our fingers in the air
of one who left something awarded
of one who knew well that death
was meritorious sane well-received
that he had served some purpose

Y ACASO ES EL FIN

hoy como se escribe poesía
simplemente meditar líneas
desembocar un océano
de agravios de muertes
y ver cuál es el resultado
crear ríos de viejas dudas
en las mejillas rosadas
en los ojos tranquilos
que se posan a ver
la televisión el cine
recordando recuperando
que el hambre la miseria
la guerra la pobreza
fue una invención de todos
sembrada bien cultivada
y meditar algo poco algo
sobre estas páginas

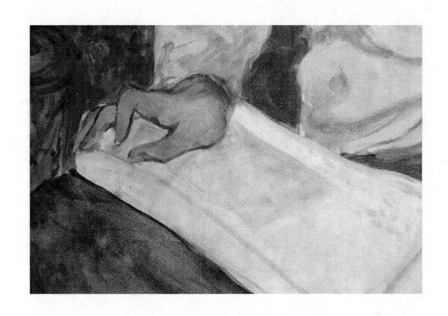

AND BY CHANCE IS THIS THE END

today as poetry is written
simply meditating lines
emptying into an ocean
of grievances of the dead
and seeing what will result
creating rivers of ancient doubts
on the rosy cheeks
the tranquil eyes
that perch to see
the television the movie
remembering recuperating
that the hunger the misery
the war the poverty
were inventions of us all
planted well cultivated
and meditating some little bit
upon these pages

BIOGRAPHIES

BENITO PASTORIZA IYODO

Benito Pastoriza Iyodo is an award-winning author from Puerto Rico. He has received various prizes in the genres of poetry and short story. The Ateneo Puertorriqueño awarded him prizes for his book of poetry *Gotas verdes para la ciudad (Green Drops for the City)* and the short story entitled "El indiscreto encanto" ("The Indiscreet Charm"). He received the Chicano Latino Literary Prize for his book of poetry entitled *Lo coloro de lo incoloro (The Color of the Colorless)*, published by the University of California. His collection of poems, *Cartas a la sombra de tu piel (Letters to the Shadow of Your Love)*, earned the prize Voces Selectas. His works have also won prizes in literary competitions in Australia, Mexico, Puerto Rico and Spain. Pastoriza was cofounder of magazines specializing in the diffusion of literature written by Latinos in the United States. The first edition of his book of short stories, *Cuestión de hombres (A Matter of Men)*, was published by The Latino Press (CUNY). His books of poetry, *Cartas a la sombra de tu piel* (2002) and *Elegías de septiembre (September Elegies)* (2003) were published by Editorial Tierra Firme in Mexico City. His second book of narratives, *Nena, nena de mi corazón (Beloved, Beloved of My Heart)*, was published by Xlibris in December of 2006. His novel, *El agua del paraíso (The Waters of Paradise)* was released in April 2008 by Xlibris. Currently the author collaborates with academic and literary magazines in the United States and abroad, which have published his interviews of distinguished poets, essays and book reviews. His writings have been published in the magazines: *En Rojo, Línea Plural, Taller Literario, Cupey, Luz en Arte y Literatura, Los Perdedores, Mystralight, Vagamundos, Carpeta de Poesía Luz, Hofstra Hispanic Review, Visible* and *Literal.* His poetry also appears in the U.S. anthologies *Poetic Voices Without Borders I and II* and in Terra Austral of Australia. The short story "Dardos en el aire" ("Darts in the Air") is included in *Uno, nosotros, todos,* an anthology published by the Spanish government's Foundation for Civil Rights. His works have been published in Australia, Mexico, Chile, Spain, Puerto Rico and the United States.

The bilingual edition of *Cuestión de hombres* titled *A Matter of Men* was published in 2008. The current collection of poetry is the second complete manuscript by Pastoriza Iyodo to be translated into English and published in bilingual format. Currently, the author is completing new projects in both poetry and fiction.

MYLES BROWN

The painter **Myles Brown** was born in Philadelphia, where he received his academic and artistic education. His paintings form part of the Paden Collection in New York City as well as the National CreataDrama Collection. Mr. Brown was awarded Art Prizes from the Carnegie Institute in Pittsburgh. His works have been displayed in galleries in Philadelphia, Pittsburgh, New York and Río de Janeiro, including several one-man shows. Myles Brown's other artistic pursuits included book illustration and stage set design. He was also a film critic and drama reviewer.

Among his best-known paintings are his Brazilian series of Bahían men and women, "The solitude of the poet," and "The poet exposed." Details from these last two paintings are highlighted in black and white as illustrations for *September Elegies*. Other drawings in the author's collection of works by Mr. Brown are included throughout this volume of poetry, as documented in the *list of illustrations*, which immediately precedes the table of contents.

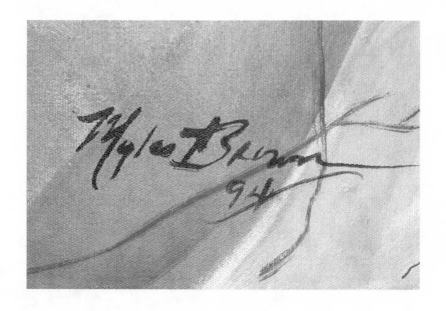

This edition is dedicated to Myles Brown.
1949-2000

BRADLEY WARREN DAVIS

One of Bradley Warren Davis's first encounters with the Spanish language and its culture occurred at an early age through a visit to Neiva, Colombia as part of a "sister city" exchange program. His fascination with the language and culture was immediate; and even though he had not yet studied Spanish, he made his first attempts at learning to communicate with his hosts. His Colombian experience, including a trip to Bogota, permitted him to observe and participate in some of the traditions of the country: their dances, music and festivals.

His second encounter with Spanish took place at Davidson College where he earned his liberal arts degree in sociology and anthropology. There he embraced the study of Spanish language and culture, taking numerous advanced courses in Spanish literature. In his sophomore year he studied in Spain where he took courses conducted in Spanish in the areas of sociology, Spanish theater and Spanish civilization. In Spain he also had the opportunity to travel throughout Andalusia, Valencia, Castile and Extremadura.

During his law school years at the University of Miami, he served as the interpreter for a group of Florida citrus specialists on a fact-finding mission to Cuba. This experience included interaction with Cuban governmental officials that accompanied the group as it traveled the island. Davis interpreted for these officials as well.

Since then Davis has incorporated Spanish into various aspects of his professional life: as a bilingual attorney; as a curriculum and bilingual materials developer and as a translator and interpreter for both Hispanic and U.S. firms. In addition, he has participated in translation symposia. His experience as a translator and interpreter has also been enriched by numerous journeys to Latin America, including: Puerto Rico, the Dominican Republic, Mexico, Costa Rica, Honduras, Nicaragua, Guatemala, Ecuador, Brazil and Venezuela.

Davis's translations have been published in newspapers, literary publications and magazines including *Arte en Luz y Literatura, Visible* and *Literal.* His poetry translation has also appeared in the U.S. anthology, *Poetic Voices Without Borders II.* Davis's first book-length translation was *A Matter of Men (Cuestión de hombres)* by Benito Pastoriza Iyodo. This bilingual edition was published in 2008 with an introduction in English, also written by the translator. Presently Davis has several translation projects being prepared for publication.

LIST OF ILLUSTRATIONS/

LISTA DE ILUSTRACIONES

INDICE

TABLE OF CONTENTS

LaVergne, TN USA
22 July 2010
190510LV00006B/70/P